PRAYER: UNWRAPPING THE GIFT

PRAYER: UNWRAPPING THE GIFT
Encouraging the local church to pray

John Preston

Contents

Introduction 7

1 Principles for corporate prayer 10

2 Individual prayer habits 16

3 Teaching resources 22

4 Developing a prayer strategy 30

5 Praying specifically 34

6 Informing prayer through research 37

7 Bringing prayer meetings to life 40

8 Praying households 44

9 Praying on location 46

10 Prayer events 54

11 Prayer for leadership 56

12 Final thoughts 59

This book is dedicated to

LISA WEST
Administrator of the Teal Trust; always patient,
encouraging yet constructive,
and to whom I owe a million thanks!

INTRODUCTION
Why corporate prayer is important

Could you imagine a DIY enthusiast receiving the latest electronic multi-purpose tool for Christmas and continuing to use a manual screwdriver? Or a car fanatic being given a fully insured Ferrari and preferring to travel in a ten-year-old wreck? When we receive gifts, our natural instinct is to want to use them to the full.

Prayer is an amazing gift from God! The Almighty Creator God promises to hear you and me whenever we turn to him. Whilst this is amazing in itself, his promise goes even further. Not only will our Father God hear our prayers, he has promised to answer them. Luke 11 records Jesus' teaching on perseverance in prayer and that the Father longs to give the power, wisdom and insight of the Holy Spirit to those who ask him. James 5:16 tells us that the prayers of righteous people are powerful and effective. Prayer makes a difference; to us and to the situations we bring before God.

Many Christians simply don't make the best use of this amazing gift. Either corporately or in our individual lives, it can be all too easy to neglect the power and potential of prayer. Even when we do seek to place prayer at the centre of our activities, sometimes we become stale and need to find new ways of praying.

Many churches believe in the critical importance of prayer. However, they struggle to find a way of practically outworking this and of developing a vibrant corporate prayer life, where members come expecting to meet with God in prayer.

This book seeks to encourage the prayer lives of our churches. It offers practical, actionable resources to make a real difference to a church's prayer life. Whilst not everything will be appropriate for every situation, we hope that at least something contained within may fire your imagination or light a spark in your heart as you read and reflect.

All of the Resource pages in this book may be copied freely for non-profit use. This permission is granted to encourage a wider discussion and to support local church teaching on corporate prayer.

We begin by providing some tools for reviewing the prayer life of a church – firstly reflection on some biblical principles for corporate intercession and then a simple template to assess elements of the church's prayer life. This is intended for use by either a leader alone or with a group.

The second chapter provides a questionnaire that has been used to explore the individual prayer habits of a number of churches. This can help build up a picture of the prayer habits of your church members, to identify teaching needs and to assess the current capacity of your church for prayer. These teaching needs are addressed in chapter Three, with the provision of two studies for house- or cell groups, as well as two sermon outlines on corporate prayer.

Churches may need to develop a conscious strategy to encourage their prayer life. Chapter Four offers tips for developing such a strategy and proposes the role of a prayer co-ordinator. Some characteristics of the right individual for this role are outlined, together with a sample job description. This book is in itself a manual for prayer co-ordinators, covering many of the resources and tools necessary to make a real difference to the role.

Being specific in our prayers is important and communicating the right information is necessary to inform prayers. Chapter Five considers how the local church can effectively communicate both the needs for prayer and answers to it, but with an appropriate degree of confidentiality. Then chapter Six explores the benefits of researching the needs of an area, developing a spiritual map of the locality and keeping a corporate prayer diary, recording significant events in the spiritual life of a community.

The next chapter proposes thirty-two ways of enlivening prayer meetings, keeping meetings fresh and ensuring that as many as possible of the church community become a part of the corporate intercessory process. A part of achieving this breadth of involvement is to encourage people to pray in their homes and with their families. This should not only be for one another and for family life but for the wider community and the church's mission to it.

The next two chapters look at taking prayer out into the life of the community, as a church or in partnership with other churches. We consider the effectiveness of prayer walking around the community, either as individuals or in organised groups and some alternative options for organised prayer events.

Our final prayer topic is seeking to ensure that our church leaders have an appropriate degree of prayer support. We provide two check-lists – firstly to help a leader review the degree of prayer support their ministry is receiving and a second for church councils or the wider church to determine whether the appropriate prayer support for the leadership of the church is in place.

CHAPTER ONE
Principles for corporate prayer

Before embarking on new ways of encouraging prayer in the local church, it is good to start with a time for reflection. First we offer eight principles that underpin corporate prayer:

1   A woven cord of many strands

When Christians pray together, the Father has a personal and unique relationship with every individual, no matter how large the group. This has two significant implications:

Firstly, our personal relationship with God is not to be compared with other people's personal relationships with God. Like a rope, greater strength in corporate prayer comes from increasing the numbers of individual thin threads, rather than by increasing the thickness of the core. In other words, one of the major tasks of the church leader in developing prayer is to encourage individuals to meet with God in prayer in a way that feels right and natural for them. They shouldn't feel that they are in a game of spiritual one-upmanship, where spiritual blessings await the most eloquently worded prayer or the person who can appear to present the most deeply spiritual issue.

For a cord to have strength, the individual strands must be woven together in a common direction. This underscores the need for agreement in prayer. In his first letter to Timothy, Paul writes: 'I want men everywhere to lift up holy hands in prayer, without anger or disputing' (1 Tim. 2:8).

In Matthew 18:19,20, we read: 'Again, I tell you that if two of you on earth agree about anything you ask for, it will be done for you by my Father in heaven. For where two or three come together in my name, there am I with them.'

The word 'agree' in this passage is *sumphoneo* in the Greek, the same source of the word symphony. A symphony consists of a wide range of instruments playing different parts, harmonising together to the same beat, to produce an overall effect much richer than any one instrumental voice.

2 Hearing God corporately

Christian experience suggests that God uses our individual gifts and relationships as channels for him to speak to a church. Very often it is through the sharing of individuals' words, thoughts and prayers that we discern the Father's will and purpose. Each of us is called to speak out what we believe God is saying, rather than to repeat what God appears to be saying to someone else. This requires confidence and an appropriate discernment process that enables members to share this with the church leadership in a discreet way.

Just as the strength of our corporate intercession can be compared to a cord of many fine threads woven together, so our corporate ear is like many individuals listening to the same conversation and then reporting back on it afterwards. Each person recalls hearing something different, which together builds a much more complete record than any one individual would have been able to produce alone.

3 Pray at all times

Acts 1:14 describes the disciples joining together 'constantly in prayer'. Acts 2:42 places prayer at the heart of the fellowship of the early believers: 'They devoted themselves to the apostles' teaching and to the fellowship, to the breaking of bread and to prayer.'

Constantly flowing intercession is unlikely to be achieved as a 'gathered church' in the average central church building, however well attended the prayer meetings may be. Rather, the corporate prayer life blends central events, with streams of prayer flowing from house to house, from group to group and from the individual prayers of church members.

4 Specifically

The Father encourages us to be specific in presenting our needs before him. Luke 11:9-13 reads

> 'So I say to you: Ask and it will be given to you; seek and you will find; knock and the door will be opened to you. For everyone who asks receives; he who seeks finds; and to him who knocks, the door will be opened.'

'Which of you fathers, if your son asks for a fish, will give him a snake instead? Or if he asks for an egg, will give him a scorpion? If you then, though you are evil, know how to give good gifts to your children, how much more will your Father in heaven give the Holy Spirit to those who ask him!'

If church members are to pray specifically, they need to know the specific needs of the church. This requires two things from the leadership. Firstly, clarity of thought is needed to define what these needs are. Secondly, clarity of communication is required for the needs to be understood by the church membership so they are able to pray effectively about them.

5 As a priority

In his first letter to Timothy, Paul allocates the very highest priority to prayer: 'I urge, then, first of all, that requests, prayers, intercession and thanksgiving be made for everyone – for kings and all those in authority, that we may live peaceful and quiet lives in all godliness and holiness' (1 Tim 2:1,2).

This passage clearly teaches that intercession is not only for ourselves or for the life of our church. It is also for our society and the context in which the church finds itself placed. Some of the great prayers in the Bible (Nehemiah 9 and Daniel 9 being two examples) are prayers of confession for the state of the nation, asking for God's mercy upon his people. Getting prayer right sets the right background for the rest of the church's mission and ministry.

6 In the right places

The geography of prayer is important. Throughout the Old Testament we read of prayer linked with territory. Where we pray makes a difference and taking prayer out of our churches and into our communities is a powerful way to pray for that area. Not only does it bring a freshness and vitality to our praying but God can use this to open our eyes to new things as we do so. It can be all too easy for prayer inside the church building to focus on the life of the church and neglect the world outside.

7   Covering the whole life of the church

What we bring to God needs to cover every aspect of our church's life, its interaction with the community we serve and the needs of the society we are a part of. If we are to combine this with praying specifically, as we discussed earlier, then there is a significant need for co-ordination, communication and deciding priorities to allow the prayer life of the church to cover these aspects properly. No one individual, not even the minister, is likely to be aware of all the wider needs for prayer unless they make a conscious effort to find them out.

8   With thanksgiving

Corporate prayer must bring not only our prayers for our needs, but also our thanks for answered prayer.

'On their release, Peter and John went back to their own people and reported all that the chief priests and elders had said to them. When they heard this, they raised their voices together in prayer to God' (Acts 4:23-24). Sharing answered prayer is as important as sharing the needs for prayer. There is nothing like answered prayer to build the capacity of that church for prayer.

Prayer Review

On the next two pages we provide a template for reviewing the corporate prayer life of your church, either alone or with others. This has been developed with two aims in mind. Firstly, it provokes some thought on corporate prayer. It may be a while since the leaders paused to reflect on the strength of corporate prayer within the church. Secondly, it provides a structured framework for some honest reflection on areas of corporate prayer that are good and working well, as well as highlighting areas which may benefit from development.

PRAYER REVIEW

First complete this on your own. Then discuss your scores with others in the church, seeking first to understand different points of view. Finally, consider the implications for developing your church's prayer life.

For each statement give a score between 1 and 4, where:

1 = Not at all true of my church.
2 = Slightly or occasionally true of my church.
3 = Often or quite true of my church.
4 = Very much true of my church.

	1	2	3	4
A woven cord of many strands				
1 Our church values different people's approaches to and experience of prayer.	☐	☐	☐	☐
2 A good proportion of church members play an active part of our corporate prayer life.	☐	☐	☐	☐
Hearing God corporately				
3 Our discernment of what God is saying to us is based on many people's perception of God's voice.	☐	☐	☐	☐
Pray at all times				
4 Our corporate prayer life is spread over the week and across the community.	☐	☐	☐	☐
Specifically				
5 Church members know the specific prayer needs leaders propose.	☐	☐	☐	☐
As a priority				
6 I feel that corporate prayer is a priority in the life of our church.	☐	☐	☐	☐
In the right place				
7 Prayer is woven into the framework of our church lives – in meetings, in homes as well as in worship times.	☐	☐	☐	☐
8 We regularly take prayer out into our community.	☐	☐	☐	☐
Covering the whole life of the church				
9 Our whole church life, our members and our community are grounded in prayer.	☐	☐	☐	☐
With thanksgiving				
10 Church members are informed of answered prayers as well as needs.	☐	☐	☐	☐

Now map out your corporate prayer life. Write down all of the events that take place in the life of your church, where you perceive there is prayer going on for the life and mission of the church or for the community you serve.

For each occasion try to think about what is prayed for. How effective is this in bringing the church's needs before God?

For example, homegroups may pray each week for the life of their group, but only occasionally for the life of the wider church. This may be largely on a particular aspect of church life, such as young people's work.

Day	Where	What is prayed For
Monday		
Tuesday		
Wednesday		
Thursday		
Friday		
Saturday		
Sunday		
Occasional events		

CHAPTER TWO
Individual prayer habits

Strong individual prayer habits amongst church members are a foundation for corporate prayer. If church members do not pray when they are alone, they are unlikely to pray effectively when they are together.

A few years ago the Teal Trust conducted a survey on individual prayer habits. Entitled *On our knees?*, it sought to gain new insights into how and when people pray, as well as what they pray for. With over 5500 completed responses from 350 churches across a range of Protestant denominations, the survey gave a comprehensive overview of the UK church at prayer and compared this with a group of churches in Australia, New Zealand and North America.

Although the background information on prayer habits was found to be extremely useful, one of the major benefits of the project was equipping 140 church leaders with a personalised report, showing the prayer habits of their church and how this compared to the national average.

With this in mind, the key results and a shortened version of the survey are included here to enable readers in church leadership positions to use this questionnaire to run a survey of their congregations. Those who aren't in leadership positions may also want to run the survey but permission of the leadership should be sought first.

Using the survey in this way will give leaders insight into the base of prayer going on in the church.

Key Findings

1 Personal prayer is important

Forty-eight per cent of respondents rated personal prayer as vital to their Christian life and faith, with a further 30% rating it as important. What respondents included in this prayer time varied widely according to personal preference and prayer style. A church's response to this question provides an important cue for teaching programmes (Chapter 3).

2 Time spent in prayer varies considerably

One third of respondents spent an hour or more in private prayer each week. Across the whole sample, respondents claimed to spend on average about seven minutes a day in private prayer.

Knowing how much time a church's membership spend praying can inform the way that prayer needs are shared (see Chapter 5).

3 There is little variation by denomination

There was relatively little variation in the pattern by denomination, except that Baptists and independent/house churches had a slightly higher proportion of people who pray for more than an hour each week.

4 Christians believe that God hears and answers prayer

The overwhelming majority believed that God hears their prayers (93%) and that they have experienced answered prayer (86%). What may be more surprising is the degree to which respondents claimed to experience two-way communication in prayer. Nearly two thirds (63%) spent time listening to God as well as talking to him and a similar number (59%) had experienced God communicating with them as they prayed.

The table below shows the difference in responses when respondents were divided into those who prayed for more than an hour and those who spent less than an hour in private prayer each week. There is also a clear link between time spent in prayer and the likelihood of reading the Bible frequently.

Those who	Less than 1 hour a week	More than 1 hour a week
% spend time listening to God	54%	80%
% experienced God communicating with them whilst they pray	49%	77%
% read the Bible every day or most days	44%	82%

5 Family and Friends is the most frequently prayed for topic

The survey asked how frequently people prayed about eleven different areas and which of these areas they spent most time praying for. The area most frequently prayed for was family and friends, with time spent thanking God close behind.

For the purposes of a review of corporate prayer, it is helpful to note the degree to which the work of the local church and church leadership are supported in prayer.

Area	Freq	Most
family/friends	89%	63%
things to thank God for	80%	28%
health/healing of particular people	67%	27%
praising and worshipping God	65%	14%
confessing things to God	58%	11%
the work of your church	44%	10%
your church leaders	41%	3%
others to come to faith (by name)	33%	8%
world/regional issues	29%	6%
others to come to faith (generally)	26%	4%
your material needs	16%	3%

6 Wandering thoughts is the biggest obstacle to prayer

The survey asked respondents to rate the degree to which five possible obstacles to prayer caused them difficulty. Wandering thoughts was found to be the biggest obstacle, with over 80% of respondents finding this at least 'sometimes a problem'. Two thirds of respondents found noise or other distractions to be a problem and just over half (54%) found finding time a barrier. The two areas that were found to be less problematic were knowing what to pray for (23%) and knowing what to say (32%)

7 Two in five Christians pray together outside church services

Eighty-four per cent of respondents agreed that 'It is important that Christians should pray together as well as alone.' However, only 39% of *On our Knees?* respondents said that they prayed with one or more people outside of church services at least once a week. A further 19% prayed with others at least once a month.

If the questionnaire is run in your church, it is worthwhile comparing the result of this question with the proportion of your church members you estimate would attend meetings and groups that include corporate prayer.

8 Just over half the respondents read their Bibles daily

Fifty-eight per cent of respondents claimed to read their Bibles either daily or most days. There was no significant difference between women (58%) and men (56%). Age also made little difference, with figures of 54% for 16 to 24 year olds, 57% for the 25-44 year old group, 58% for the 45 to 64 year olds and 57% for the over 65 year olds.

There was a clear link between the frequency of Bible reading and the amount of time spent in prayer. Eighty-nine per cent of those praying for more than two hours a week will read their Bibles either daily or on most days. Only 26% of those praying for less than fifteen minutes a week will read their Bible daily.

PRAYER QUESTIONNAIRE

This questionnaire is intended to help the church leadership understand more about the corporate prayer life of the church. Please answer as honestly as you can. All answers are anonymous.

Please put a ✔ in the appropriate boxes

Section 1 About Your Prayer Life

1 How often do you pray alone, outside of church services?

Every day	☐	Once or twice a month	☐
Most days	☐	Less often	☐
Once or twice a week	☐	Never	☐

2 How often do you pray with one or more other people, excluding church services?

Every day	☐	Once or twice a month	☐
Most days	☐	Less often	☐
Once or twice a week	☐	Never	☐

3 How often do you read the Bible (excluding homegroups or Sunday services) ?

Every day	☐	Once or twice a month	☐
Most days	☐	Less often	☐
Once or twice a week	☐	Never	☐

Section 2 : When you pray alone

1 How important is personal prayer time to your Christian life and faith?

Unimportant ☐   Fairly important ☐   Important ☐   Vital ☐

2 Which of the following do you find to be obstacles to prayer ?

	Not a problem	Sometimes a problem	Frequently a problem	A major obstacle
I can't seem to find time	☐	☐	☐	☐
I don't know what to pray for	☐	☐	☐	☐
I don't know what to say	☐	☐	☐	☐
I find my thoughts wandering	☐	☐	☐	☐
Noise or other distractions	☐	☐	☐	☐

3 In your private prayer, how often do you pray about or pray for

	Frequently	Sometimes	Occasionally	Never
a family/friends	☐	☐	☐	☐
b the health/healing of particular people	☐	☐	☐	☐
c world or regional issues	☐	☐	☐	☐
d your material needs	☐	☐	☐	☐
e the work of your church	☐	☐	☐	☐
f your church leaders	☐	☐	☐	☐
g for others to come to faith (generally)	☐	☐	☐	☐
h for others to come to faith (by name)	☐	☐	☐	☐
i things you want to thank God for	☐	☐	☐	☐
j praising and worshipping God	☐	☐	☐	☐
k things you want to confess to God	☐	☐	☐	☐

4 Over the past week, how much time in total did you spend in quiet personal prayer (excluding time spent in services or saying a daily office)?

under 5 mins ☐	30 mins to 1 hr ☐	over 5 hrs ☐
5 to 15 mins ☐	1 to 2 hours ☐	
15 to 30 mins ☐	2 to 5 hours ☐	

Section 3: What do you think about prayer?

For each statement below, please circle **1** if you strongly disagree, **2** if you disagree, **3** if you neither agree nor disagree, **4** if you agree and **5** if you strongly agree.

1 I believe God hears my prayers

        1   *2*   *3*   *4*   *5*

2 I spend time listening to God as well as talking to him

        1   *2*   *3*   *4*   *5*

3 I have experienced prayer being answered

        1   *2*   *3*   *4*   *5*

4 I have experienced God communicating with me as I pray

        1   *2*   *3*   *4*   *5*

5 I feel comfortable praying aloud with others

        1   *2*   *3*   *4*   *5*

6 I would like to receive more teaching on prayer

        1   *2*   *3*   *4*   *5*

CHAPTER THREE
Teaching resources

Diversity within the local church makes developing an effective teaching programme on prayer extremely challenging. In addition to the usual challenges of diversity of Christian experience and preferred learning styles, differences in individual spiritualities add an additional complication.

Yet without an effective teaching programme, our strategy reverts to the default approach; that somehow people will work out for themselves why it is important to pray and how to do it. No matter how sincere the desire of people to pray, if they lack the basic skills, as well as the understanding of fundamental principles on prayer, they are unlikely to pray effectively over a period of time.

Homegroups

As well as learning to pray by themselves, new disciples (and some older ones!) may benefit from reflecting on why it is critical that Christians also pray with others. Whilst there are a good number of books and Bible study resources around on individual prayer, there are far fewer available on praying in groups.

Thus in this chapter we present two discussion outlines for homegroups. The first provides a basic introduction to Jesus' teaching on prayer and why it applies both to our prayer lives as individuals and in groups. This is based around the teaching in Luke 11 on the Lord's Prayer. The second study is based on the first and final chapters of the letter of James.

A homegroup is a good place to encourage people to learn to pray. It should be a safe environment, where relationships have been built up. Further, bringing prayer into the life of the group will enable members to share their concerns with the Lord. If prayer is a part of the regular life of a homegroup, then the leaders or the group may like to spend ten minutes considering the following three review questions:

1 What one or two things about our prayer time would we identify as really working?

2 What would we like to do differently? Be specific about what you would like to change and how.

3 What answered prayer can we identify? Do we regularly give thanks to God together for answered prayer?

Whole church teaching

Pause for a moment and think back over the sermon programme for the last year or two – identifying where teaching on prayer was included. Then move on to think about the needs of your congregation. The needs for teaching on prayer will differ between seekers, new converts and more mature disciples, but nevertheless all of these groups need appropriate teaching which enables them to develop their prayer lives.

Some preachers may feel inadequate preaching on prayer. This may be particularly true if they feel that their prayer life is not all that it could be. However, it is quite likely that our prayer lives will never be all that they could be! Thus it may simply be necessary to preach on the basis of what the Bible teaches and acknowledge that at times we struggle to live up to this.

Here are some possible themes for whole church teaching :

- *Luke 18:1-8*   Persistent prayer (outline provided)
- *Matthew 18:15-20*   When two or three agree (outline provided)
- *James 1 and 5*   Praying with faith (as Bible Study outline)
- *Matthew 6:5-14*   Praying the words Jesus gave
- *Romans 8*   Praying with the Spirit within us
- *Nehemiah 9*   Confessing and asking for grace
- *1 Timothy 2:1-8*   Interceding for the world
- *Ephesians 6*   Praying in the spiritual battle
- *Daniel 9*   Praying into the promise, mercy and glory of God

Why not ask members of the congregation about the aspects of prayer on which they would like to receive some teaching?

HOME STUDY OUTLINE 1: WHAT DO YOU EXPECT?

Introduction: Think for a moment of some of the prayers you have prayed. Do you think some of your prayers are more likely to be answered than others? If so, which?

Read Luke 11: 1-13 together

1 The disciples asked Jesus to teach them to pray. How did you learn to pray?

2 When we pray, we might see God as 'Father' (vv11-13) or as 'Lord' or 'God' or something else. How does seeing God as Father help us to ask for things?

3 Do you think the man's request was reasonable?

4 Do our prayers need to be 'reasonable' or does verse 10 mean we can ask for anything we want?

5 Consider verses 11 to 13. What do these verses teach us about what we should expect from God when we pray?

6 What do you think Jesus means when he says 'give the Holy Spirit to those who ask him'?

7 Notice that in the Lord's prayer, Jesus uses 'we' language: 'Our Father' (some versions), 'give us each day', 'forgive us' etc. Do you see prayer as being mainly an individual or a group thing?

8 What kind of prayers do you find easiest to pray in a group and what prayers do you find easiest to pray alone?

9 Do you think it makes a difference whether a prayer is prayed by a group or by an individual?

10 What are your priorities for prayer as a group right now? End your time together by praying these through together.

HOME STUDY OUTLINE: NOTES FOR LEADERS

Q1 For some, the idea of learning to pray will be new. Yet the disciples knew that they needed to be taught to pray.

Q2 Galatians 4:6 tells us that 'because you are sons, God sent the Spirit of his Son into our hearts, the Spirit who calls out "Abba"' (Aramaic for Father, Dad). In verses 11-13, the snake and the scorpion may refer to evil things (see Lk. 10:18,19).

Jesus is not saying in this passage that the Father is like the reluctant friend. Rather, he is saying, 'how much more' will the Father want to answer. The Father-child relationship is a cornerstone for prayer – we come in simplicity as children to a loving parent.

Q4 Some groups will want to explore this question at length. Key discussion points may include how God will answer 'unreasonable' prayer, reasons for unanswered prayer and praying 'in Jesus' name' (Jn.16:23).

Q6 Matthew's version has 'give good gifts' (Mt 7:11) meaning the gifts of the Holy Spirit. The Holy Spirit is God's greatest gift to us – the presence of himself within us.

Q7 Prayer is clearly both an individual and a corporate activity. Many will find it easiest to begin by developing an individual prayer life before being willing to open up in prayer in a group context.

Q9 Praying together takes us into the principle of agreement. Matthew 18:19,20 says 'If two of you on earth agree about anything you ask for, it will be done by my Father in heaven.' This gives us a clear reason for group prayer. Also the practical benefit of the woven cord principle (page 8) suggests that as different people pray, their prayers bind and blend together. However, for many people, there will be certain more personal concerns which we only feel comfortable praying about in private.

HOME STUDY OUTLINE 2:
PERSEVERING PRAYER

Introduction: Think of a difficult moment in your life when you turned to prayer. What difference did praying make?

Read James 1:1-8

1   Do we consider it pure joy when we experience trials of many kinds? If not, why not?

2   The response James recommends to the hardship being encountered by his readers is to increase their faith. How does faith help us face difficulties?

3   Verse 3 encourages us to ask for wisdom to deal with the hardship, rather than for a particular solution to the hardship itself. Would we rather pray for the solution or for wisdom?

4   Verses 5 to 8 speak about trusting God to answer our prayer for wisdom. What helps us to do this?

Read James 2:14-18

5   James teaches that faith and deeds are linked. What does this mean in the context of prayer?

6   Have you been used in the answer to your own prayer? If so, when?

Read James 5:13-18

7   James ends by referring to the power of prayer. What topics do you pray for when you are on your own?

8   This teaching is clearly in the context of group or church prayer. For what kind of things do you pray in groups? If this is different to the previous question, why do you think this is?

9   Verse 15 talks about 'the prayer offered in faith'. What kinds of prayer do you find it easiest to have faith in? Why?

10 End the session by firstly praising God, then praying for any troubles amongst the group (v13). Finally pray for the wisdom of the Spirit for one another (1:5).

HOME STUDY OUTLINE 2: NOTES FOR LEADERS

Q1 It is almost impossible for many of us to consider trials 'pure joy' at the time. James teaches us to recognise the positive effects trials can produce in our lives; faith, learning and perseverance (See also Rom. 5:2-5).

Q3 Wisdom is not about knowledge, but about the ability to make good decisions. As the Holy Spirit leads us (see Lk. 11:13) we gain God's perspective on issues.

Q4 We trust God on the basis of Scripture, supported by our own experience. God's faithfulness in previous trials (either our own or others), brings the 'heart and soul' evidence that combines with the 'mind' evidence of reading God's word.

'Double minded' refers to placing our trust in both God and the world – we cannot have it both ways. If we place our trust in God, we do not need another option. If we are relying on a second option, then we are hoping God will answer, not trusting that he will.

Q5 & 6 Being a disciple of Jesus Christ requires upwards faith and outwards action. We are saved by faith (Rom. 3:22) and the deeds flow from this. Linking this to prayer, we are called to pray for the world and those around us, but we are also called to respond with practical expressions of love.

Q7 The prayer survey in Chapter Two gives a list of the kind of topics people pray for (see p14). This question does not intend that people should share specific details of their prayers but rather the broad groups to encourage one another to pray about a wide range of issues.

Q9 Praying in faith is not so much about having certainty in how God will answer the prayer, but placing our trust in the Father's character and nature. The Father is generous and has good things to give. The righteous (v16) are not the spiritual élite but rather those who put their trust in God.

SERMON OUTLINE 1: PERSISTENT PRAYER

Text: Luke 18:1-8

Note the parable's purpose is so important it is actually presented in the text.

Four principles for persistence:

i Don't be put off by the standards of the world

The judge has no concern for God or the needs of others.
The widow would have had no access to him. Attendants would bring cases to him, often as the result of a bribe.

ii Don't give up when times are hard

The widow is likely to be poor so couldn't bribe the unjust judge.
She has no husband to present her case for her. She has an unjust adversary yet she appeals persistently.

iii Keep on keeping on

Eventually the judge was persuaded to act – to preserve his own sanity. How much more does God want to respond to our needs?
A delay in seeing the answer is not the same as no answer from God. God's support and care is instantaneous, but the response will be in his timing. For him, one day is as a thousand years – and vice versa.

iv Our faith in Christ and his faith in us

Verse 8 looks forward to the second coming. There is a time of decline and persecution assumed in Revelation. Persistence will be needed. Faith in him is rewarded – the centurion didn't need Jesus to come to his house (Lk. 7): 'Just say the word.'
Yet also Christ places faith in us. The church was established with twelve disciples. Jesus taught them how to pray. So we too carry on the work of building the Kingdom and of praying.

Application

■ Know what our prayer needs are and keep on praying.

■ Share needs with others so we can share the burden.

■ Listen as persistently as we pray!

SERMON OUTLINE 2: WHEN TWO OR THREE AGREE

Text: Matthew 18:15-20 and Hebrews 10:19-25

Matthew 18:20 – Where two or three come together in Christ's name, he is there with them. So how do we act when we are together?

i Help one another to live out the Gospel (Mt)

The first responsibility we have to each other is to share our Christian life. We need to help each other with sinfulness, initially in private (v15). We should do this only when we have forgiven the other person (see the following parable) so that no anger remains. Jesus teaches us that we should do this in a brother-sister relationship, not teacher-pupil. And we have a responsibility to listen to others who confront us with our sin (v15).

ii Encourage one another (Heb)

Encourage in both our faith and in doing good works.
Draw close to God with sincere heart – it's for him, not us!
Example of encouraging from personal experience?

iii Keep on meeting together (Heb)

We need to be committed to meeting together and to seeing ourselves as the family of God – brothers and sisters, not acquaintances we hardly know.

iv Agreement (Mt)

Whatever we agree on in prayer, God will answer. How the prayer is answered is for God, not us. We lift the situation and ask for God's Spirit to intervene; rather than recommending the best solution for God to adopt!
'The biggest problem in prayer is how to let go and let God' (Glenn Clark). When we are sick and go to a doctor, we present the problem and ask him/her to help us. We don't often prescribe how to help! Thus it should be with God, who has so much more of the full picture than we imagine could possibly exist.

Application

- How do we meet together: twos and threes, homegroups?

- When we pray together, do we know the presence of Christ among us? How do we recognise this presence?

- When we ask, we must ask in faith, believing God answers prayer.

CHAPTER FOUR
Developing and implementing a prayer strategy

Corporate prayer is like a tender perennial flower rather than an invasive weed. It needs focus, time and care for it to grow. Left to itself, the corporate prayer life of a church is likely to wither and die. Church leaders have a key role in developing the capacity of the church for prayer, either by personal attention or by recruiting and enabling a prayer co-ordinator.

Some leaders will choose to develop the prayer life of their church in a relatively unstructured way. This is fine, as long as unstructured doesn't mean neglected! However, some may prefer to add some structure through a clear strategy to encourage the development of certain elements of the corporate prayer life.

A prayer strategy should be a short document, with only a few bullet points, that outlines how a church plans to develop its prayer life and ensure that prayer needs are adequately covered. It is best put together by a church council or leadership team, arising from a review of the prayer life of the church. Like any strategy, it will need to identify people who will be responsible for ensuring that the required action happens.

This prayer strategy is likely to be broad, encompassing both existing prayer groups and other future opportunities. It should consider all of the places where prayer is happening in the life of the church. It would also benefit from linking into the corporate teaching and preaching programme, to ensure that the individual prayer lives of church members are being nourished.

A thorough review of the prayer life of a church is an excellent way of beginning the process of developing such a strategy. It then becomes possible to identify ways of encouraging further growth in what is already going on and also spotting the 'gaps'. The tool in Chapter One can form an agenda for such a review, taking an evening or whole day meeting for a leadership team.

AN EXAMPLE OF A PRAYER STRATEGY

Bingham Community Church Prayer Plan

We value prayer highly and plan:

- **to increase our prayer time** – by holding a weekly prayer group, by encouraging all our housegroups to include some time in prayer at each meeting and by encouraging people to have a daily personal quiet time with God.

- **to pray for our leaders, our mission and ministry** by giving prayer needs in each Sunday's newsletter and by holding half-day prayer meetings every three months.

- **to provide regular teaching on prayer** on Sunday mornings.

- **to respond quickly to urgent prayer requests** from church members via a prayer team co-ordinator, available 24 hours a day, who will pass such requests on to our prayer network via e-mail.

A good prayer strategy document:

IS SPECIFIC – readers will know exactly what the church is going to do.

MAKES CHOICES – doesn't try to do everything at once, but decides on priorities and makes progress against them.

IS ACHIEVABLE – it is much better to aim for a realistic amount and achieve it, than aim for the impossible and fail.

Appointing a prayer co-ordinator

Developing and implementing a prayer strategy takes time and focus. It is best achieved by appointing an individual who can make this their primary ministry. This is an important role and one that will take a considerable amount of time. It is probably best not to add this on top of someone's existing commitments, but rather to reflect on whether God may be leading them in this new direction for a period, at the expense of some existing areas of ministry.

In selecting a prayer co-ordinator, the most deeply prayerful church member may not be the best candidate. The skills required are more to do with co-ordination, effective communication and encouraging others, rather than just personal prayerfulness. Whilst the prayer co-ordinator should not be seen as the church's prayer expert, it is clear that the prayer co-ordinator should be passionate about prayer and hold prayer to be an essential part of their personal walk of faith.

If done well, the job of prayer co-ordinator will be a complex one, linking with many other areas of the church's life. It is therefore important to define the role and producing a job description encourages clarity. The roles listed provide a good place to start, although not every prayer co-ordinator's role would necessarily feature all of these!

Ideally the co-ordinator will have a number of personal attributes as well as skills. They will need to be able to manage confidentiality, to make good decisions as to which prayer needs are released to which groups of people and also about the level of detail that is provided with these prayer needs. This requires wisdom and judgement. The prayer co-ordinator will also require good interpersonal skills in order to be able to pull together the church's pattern of prayer.

When such a prayer co-ordinator is appointed, they will need regular time with the leadership. Brief communication will be required fairly frequently as individual prayer needs arise, but it is vital to build in longer discussions on a regular basis. This helps to take an overview of what God might be saying to the church, to review the strategy and to discuss issues that may be arising.

Prayer co-ordinator role

The role of prayer co-ordinator could include some or all of the following:

- Working with the church's leadership to develop and implement a prayer strategy.

- Facilitating the flow of information for people to be able to pray effectively.

- Editing and producing a prayer diary.

- Recruiting people willing to pray for specific prayer requests that are fed into the church.

- Encouraging the corporate prayer life by working with homegroup leaders.

- Co-ordinating prayer meetings across the church's life. This may or may not include the responsibility of leading some of these meetings.

- Producing and issuing prayer bulletins by e-mail to provide the specific details necessary for church members to pray effectively.

- Working with those responsible for preaching and teaching to ensure that a regular focus on prayer topics is built into the church's teaching programme.

- Leading the development of occasional prayer events such as prayer breakfasts or half nights of prayer.

- Pulling together a summary of what God may be saying to the church in that particular place. The prayer co-ordinator does not need to provide the ultimate discernment of whether this is right, merely to pull it together.

CHAPTER FIVE
Praying specifically

The Bible is clear that we should pray specifically, boldly and persistently. Yet we also need to pray according to God's direction. Jesus taught the disciples to pray persistently. Luke 11: 5-8 says

> 'Suppose one of you has a friend and he goes to him at midnight and says, "Friend, lend me three loaves of bread, because a friend of mine on a journey has come to me and I have nothing to set before him." Then the one inside answers, "Don't bother me. The door is already locked and my children are with me in bed. I can't get up and give you anything." I tell you, though he will not get up and give him the bread because he is his friend, yet because of the man's boldness (or persistence) he will get up and give him as much as he needs.'

There are several reasons why God wants us to pray in this way:

i   When we pray generally, we are never really sure whether God has answered our prayer. But when we pray specifically, we can see the evidence of answered prayer. This grows and develops our faith, strengthens our prayer lives and God is glorified.

ii As we pray, God wants to see whether or not we are serious about the things we ask. If we are half-hearted in what we ask, then our prayers are much less likely to be answered.

iii This links with our degree of faith. The Gospel accounts reveal a number of examples where Jesus' healing miracles are linked to the faith of the person who was healed or the faith of those who brought the situation to Jesus.

iv As we are bold and specific in prayer, it can be easier for God to use us in responding to that prayer. For example, Nehemiah prayed specifically for the opportunity to help rebuild the walls of Jerusalem. God gave him the opportunity to present his case to the king and permission was granted for Nehemiah to go and carry out the work.

Communicating Prayer Needs

One of the barriers preventing people praying effectively for their church and their community is a lack of knowledge of what to pray for. Leaving people to work it out for themselves is fine for some more mature Christians but there will be many who will pray more effectively if they are given some guidance as to what to pray for.

One of the challenges in communicating prayer needs is to match the amount of communication to the needs of those who are praying. The pyramid model below may be helpful.

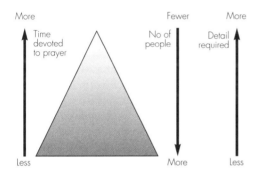

This model suggests that the majority of church members will devote relatively little time to prayer and will need correspondingly less information to guide their prayers.

A middle group may exist, willing to spend more time praying for their church. They will have greater needs for information. Finally there may be a much smaller group of intercessors, people willing to spend a significant amount of time praying for their church and community. These people are likely to require much more information and may well have responses to pass back from their prayer times.

The following page gives seven methods for communicating prayer, with a suggestion of which of the above groups that method is most appropriate for. Each church does not need to use all seven methods, but it may be helpful to review how well the information needs of each group of prayers are met.

Information for prayer needs should follow the 'STAR' mnemonic:

- Specific
- Timely
- In Appropriate detail (maintaining confidentiality)
- Relevant

SEVEN CHANNELS FOR COMMUNICATING PRAYER

1 **Weekly service sheet**: this could include one or more suggested prayer topics for the week, forthcoming events or the names of those who have asked for prayer (all groups).

2 **Prayer diary**: producing a prayer diary on a regular basis can give those who are prepared to pray regularly a focus for each day or each week. This diary could include particular areas of church life; streets in the community, parts of the church's vision, key leaders, community needs or mission areas (middle tier and intercessors).

3 **Prayer e-bulletin**: where a good number of church members have Internet access, email is a great way of rapidly distributing a prayer need amongst the church community. It can be much more effective than a telephone prayer chain. The only drawback is the speed with which emails can be forwarded and the potential risk to confidentiality (middle tier and intercessors).

4 **Prayer web page**: having a page of the church's website dedicated to current prayer topics allows the casual browser to join in the prayer life of the church. This can give both background detail to aid the prayer and answers to prayer (all groups).

5 **Prayer focus for the month**: announce a particular prayer focus for each month, using the notices slot at Sunday worship to introduce it (broad church and middle tier).

6 **Parish magazine**: this can be an additional way of communicating a prayer diary for the coming month – providing topics for each day or for each week (broad church and middle tier).

7 **Prayer briefings**: for those who are intercessors willing to spend several hours praying through a topic, it may be well worth briefing them properly. After all, if church members pursuing other ministries were to undergo a task, they would expect to be briefed. Doing it face to face also allows feedback from previous prayer (intercessors).

CHAPTER SIX
Informing prayer through research

In the last chapter we explored the principle of praying specifically. Spending time doing some background research can really help identify the specific prayer needs of a particular area.

The aim of the research is twofold. At a high level, it can inform the choice of priorities for prayer. It can also provide the background details to enable those praying to do so specifically. It is equivalent to the intelligence function of an army preparing to go into battle – again at both the strategic and tactical level. Strategically, intelligence aids the high-level battle plan, making sure the troops are committed in the right place. Tactically, intelligence provides detail to those in the field.

Whilst it is good to undertake some basic research before doing any form of prayer walking (see Chapter Nine), it is vital if you are making a longer-term commitment to pray for an area. God can use the time spent in research as powerfully as he can use the time spent in prayer.

Spiritual mapping is a useful tool to match particular insights to geographic localities. Page 39 at the end of this chapter has three ways of developing such maps; covering people, events and prayer results. Each gives a complementary dimension to support prayer walking and other ways of praying for an area.

Demographic facts and figures: your local library is likely to be able to provide you with an overview of the demography of your area – how it compares with the national average or with other local areas. This will give you some basic statistics that provide a level of insight into some of the needs of your community.

Housing analysis: what can you observe from the housing in the area? How are house prices changing? What types of people are moving in or out? What impact is this having on the local population? This will be largely observational, but local estate agents may be able to give you some insight into how things are changing.

Work: who are the major employers of people living around you? What are the pressures facing people working there? What level of unemployment is there? Is the area prospering economically?

Leisure: where do local people spend their time and money? What shops are there around you? What local facilities do you have: sports centres, pubs, eating places, parks, footpaths, community halls and play areas?

You may find it useful to compile a folder to keep all your research together. After all, if you were going on a major holiday or changing a car, it is likely that you would gather some research to inform your decision. So why not apply it to your praying for your community?

Resources to inform prayer research

1   MAPS: Ordnance survey maps, town street maps, maps on the web e.g. www.streetmap.co.uk; www.easymap.co.uk

2   LOCAL NEWSPAPERS: not just the news pages, but look at other pages as well e.g. sport, events, adverts and announcements.

3   NEWSLETTERS AND MAGAZINES: not only the church magazine, but newsletters from other organisations – what is happening? What are their issues? etc. You may want to follow this up by talking to some of the organisations' leaders. Many people expect prayer to be one of the functions of the local church and welcome the support.

4   PARISH OR LOCAL COUNCIL REPORTS: whilst some of the issues may be of little interest, councils will also discuss a number of fundamental community issues. Talking to local leaders about the issues facing the community will provide some good food for prayer.

5   LIBRARY RESEARCH: the Office of National Statistics publish a number of statistics arising from the census, which give an overall indication of how a particular locality compares with the national picture. You may be aware of much of this but there may be some interesting prayer points arising from it.

SPIRITUAL MAPPING

1   Get a large-scale map or plan of your area.

2   On this mark key buildings: churches, schools, hospitals etc.

3   Plot where your church members live with a red dot. If you can, add Christians from other churches. This will give you an overview of where the Christians are. If you have any prayer groups/house groups or praying households, add them to your map in a different colour.

4   Over time, add to this map three things (you can either make multiple copies of the map or use different colours!)

   a   *Map the contact the church has with people in this area.* This is not particularly about keeping detailed records on the lives of individuals, which could be felt to be intrusive. Rather, it is a measure of the degree of success that the church is having in making contact with people in different parts of the community and helps identify how God is responding to prayers for outreach in this area.

   b   *Map events and happenings.* Noting crime, accidents, tragic family news and other incidents can help build up a different picture of the spiritual needs of an area. This map may take several months or years to develop, but is hugely useful to those wanting to make a long-term commitment to praying for an area.

   c   *Map out the results of prayer walking the area.* As you and other people walk and pray throughout the area, what do you feel God saying about a particular place? You may also want to add to this map answered prayer results. Again, this map will take time to build up but can yield some fascinating insights to support ongoing prayer.

CHAPTER SEVEN
Bringing prayer meetings to life

This chapter is primarily aimed at church leaders and those responsible for leading a prayer group. Prayer groups can be highly effective ways of keeping the church in tune with the leading of God's Spirit and ensuring that the life and ministry of the church is fully supported in prayer. Alternatively they can be dry sessions, attended by the faithful few out of a sense of duty. Experiences of the vitality and freshness of the renewing presence of God are then a dim and distant memory. Ask yourself the question; what do you believe would be the effect on your church if your prayer group(s) ceased to exist?

Church prayer groups need encouragement and leadership if they are not to lose their direction. Here are thirty two ideas that may help to keep the group fresh and focused.

Prayer meetings need some of the fundamentals of good meeting practice...

1   What's the **purpose** of the prayer meeting? We wouldn't think of holding a meeting without being clear what we are trying to achieve in it. Thus with the prayer meeting – what's it for?

2   Who's **leading** it? Whilst openness to the Holy Spirit is important and it is good to allow the Spirit to change the tack the group might have otherwise taken, nevertheless a lack of leadership and direction can lead to drifting minds.

3   So what's the **agenda**? Having some form of structure with a clear move from one topic to another can be useful. This shouldn't be timed so tightly that there is no room for being open to consider different topics as the Spirit moves. Sensitive leadership should give people a steer as to where the group is going.

4   This may require the leader to do some **preparation**!

5   Keeping minutes may be a little formal, but having some record, such as a **prayer diary**, can help the group appreciate answered prayer and discern what God may be saying to the group.

6   Sometimes prayer groups can have action steps! God may choose to answer the prayer through those present.

Preparing to lead

7   **Spend time in quiet prayer**, listening to God to discover the things he has on his agenda.

8   **Gain input from others** as to what they feel are the major prayer topics for the meeting. Together you may have greater discernment about what you should be praying for.

9   **Plan the time** by dividing the meeting into a number of broad sections, each with a particular focus. This will enable you to ensure that the meeting covers all of the major points identified above.

10   Think through how you will **introduce each section**. Use news items, statistics, objects or passages of Scripture appropriately, but ensure that you don't take so long introducing an item that there is little time left for prayer.

11   When introducing topics, consider using some form of **visual aid** to help people remember the prayer points as they pray. These could include handouts, PowerPoint slides, a flip chart, maps or an object.

12   Make a **short video** of particular aspects of church life or the community to introduce the prayer. This is especially good where the prayer is focusing on a topic that many of the group will know little about.

Seven tips for participants

Those with responsibility for leading a prayer group need to adopt certain behaviours if the group is to be effective. So do those participating!

13   **Be actively involved** with the prayers – by both praying silently in your heart along with the topics being raised and by being willing to pray aloud.

14   **Watch your language!** Some prayers are in such eloquent language they seem designed to impress others in the group rather than God. Even if that isn't the intention, they can make it harder for newcomers to pray. It

is also better to pray briefly several times during the meeting than once at length.

15 When you pray ensure **other members of the group can hear your prayers**. This makes it possible for them to pray with you in their hearts and to say 'Amen' with some idea of what they are responding to!

16 The prayers of the group should be **a cord of individual strands** – each blending with and building on the prayers prayed previously rather than bouncing from one topic to another.

17 When you pray, **be as specific as you can** in your request and stay focused on that request. Sometimes people can wander across a range of unconnected subjects, making it hard for people to continue praying afterwards.

18 **Try to discern what God's will is** for a situation and let this guide your prayer. We can bring our heartfelt needs and desires before the Lord. Whilst it is an amazing promise that the Almighty Creator of the universe will hear and respond, he is God and works according to his Sovereign will.

19 Don't just pray, **be willing to be used** to answer the prayer.

Breaking into small groups

20 In longer meetings, **change the size/structure of the groups** every ten to twelve minutes or with each new section of prayer.

21 It can be good to **alternate between different sizes of groups**, but these should number no more than seven or eight people since it becomes hard to hear what different people are praying. Spending time praying in twos and threes provides a good balance to time praying in fours or sixes, where people are comfortable with this.

22 **Different topics** can be allocated to different groups. For instance, if you are praying for an area of your community, different groups could take different roads or different groups of people e.g. the elderly, youth, commuters, etc.

Keeping it fresh

23 **Pray on location** – go into the room you use for your young people's groups to pray for them or into the main church building to pray for your worship.

24 **Pray around the community** as well as in the church building (see Chapter 10).

25 **Change the time and place** of the meeting from time to time to enable fresh people to come.

26 Consider having **special meetings** to pray for particular topics or areas of ministry, as this may draw people with an interest in that area of ministry to that prayer meeting. This will broaden the number of people who join in the church's corporate prayer life.

27 **Change the style of prayer**. For example, consider using a graffiti prayer wall for people to jot down prayer topics.

28 Alternatively have a number of **prayer stations** around the room, each focusing on a particular topic. Allow people to move around these stations, praying for that topic at each place and then moving on.

29 **Forty day groups**. Encouraging people to pray about a particular topic for forty days is a great way of bringing some special focus onto a current need of the church.

30 **Virtual prayer groups** need not meet at a particular time and place but can be a group of people committing to each other to pray through a topic in their own homes. They may benefit from a prayer guide with regular updates and should get together from time to time to share with one another.

31 Include **worship** and individual reflection as a part of the prayer session. Allow time listening to God as well as talking to him.

32 **Enjoy meeting with God!** Prayer isn't meant to be boring or irrelevant.

CHAPTER EIGHT
Praying Households

Households offer a fantastic opportunity to bring prayer into the localities in which we live. Whether a house is a family praying, a group of Christians living together, the meeting place of a church homegroup or simply Christian friends gathering together to pray for their neighbourhood, this is a powerful way of bringing our communities and their needs before God.

The Praying Households scheme first started in India, where Mission India planted 100,000 'witnessing prayer cells' in the first ten years of the scheme. The idea has since spread to the UK, the USA and many other places. This is also a great way for churches to take their prayer ministry out into the communities they serve. If leaders choose to run this scheme, it is helpful to provide some guidance to your praying households on what you are aiming to achieve by the 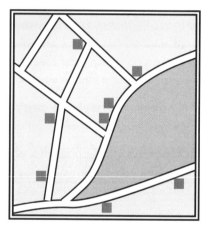 scheme and what they should be praying for. With just a few households joining the scheme, an area can effectively be covered in prayer (see diagram).

The Praying Households scheme can also be a great opportunity for churches within an area to collaborate. This is likely to increase the density of Christians living in a particular area and can enable more praying households to be formed. It also strengthens the principle of agreement, with all church communities coming together in prayer for an area which they have a shared mission to serve.

The role of the prayer co-ordinator can be extremely useful in encouraging individual households to form, facilitating ongoing communication of prayer needs and recording answered prayer.

POINTERS FOR PRAYING HOUSEHOLDS

Here are some thoughts on what to pray for:

1 Pray for your **immediate neighbours**, for example, seven households around where you are living. If you don't know their names, then find out! Pray for them specifically, for any needs that you are aware of. If they are not Christians, then pray that they may want to find out more about Jesus. If you don't know much about them and their needs, you may like to have an open house where you can invite them in for coffee or a barbeque.

2 Pray for the **particular needs of your community**; for schools, community life and those who are working in the community. Each area has its own specific needs and issues and the praying households scheme allows focused prayer to be brought to bear on these local issues.

3 Pray for the **wider community**; for your town, city or county council and the broader issues within your area. Pray particularly for those with leadership roles in your community and for the church's ministry and working relationships with these people. Relationships between church and local government can take a while to develop, so this is a long-term prayer need. Again, you may need to do some research to inform your prayers.

4 Finally, pray for **your household**, that you may continue to be a good witness in the community and for any specific needs amongst those praying. Pray that you would have the time and energy to help establish Christian community in your area.

5 As the scheme develops, pray for **other praying households**, especially those close to you. You might like to meet with them occasionally to pray together and encourage each other.

CHAPTER NINE
Praying on location

An area can be covered with prayer in three ways:

1   From the centre – through the prayers of the gathered community in church.

2   By the prayers of church members in their homes, either informally or through a network of praying households (see the previous chapter). Praying households are an excellent way of establishing prayer points around your area. Different households or groups of Christians make a commitment to pray regularly for their immediate area.

3. Taking prayer out into an area, either by individuals and groups prayer-walking the area or by running specific prayer meetings and events at particular locations.

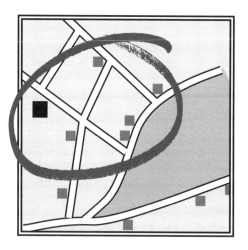

The above plan shows a central church building (large square) with a number of praying households scattered throughout the area it serves (small squares). The circled area is the church's focus for prayer walking for the coming month and this focus is likely to move from area to area over time.

Prayer Walking

Prayer walking has been part of our Christian heritage for many centuries. The British countryside has many long distance paths that were used centuries ago by monks and other travellers, moving from one cathedral city to another. Prayer walking today still has the power to take our prayer out into the territory around us. Just as many British churches had an ancient tradition of 'beating the bounds', during which they would lay claim to their parish for God, so too prayer walking today can claim territory for Christ.

The Bible links walking with God's promises on several occasions; Noah is described as 'walking with God' (Gen. 6:9), Abraham was told to 'Go, walk through the length and breadth of the land, for I am giving it to you' (Gen. 13:17). Joshua was told, 'I will give every place where you set your foot as I promised Moses' (Josh. 1:3). The prophet Micah declared, 'All the nations may walk in the name of their gods; we will walk in the name of the Lord our God for ever and ever' (Mich. 4:5).

Developing the habit of prayer walking enables us to see our neighbourhoods as Christ sees them and allows us to offer up prayers for things we see. As we prayer walk the streets of our villages, towns and cities, the Holy Spirit can give us his insight into the spiritual climate around us. Such insight can have a powerful effect on our mission and ministry strategies.

Prayer walking can be used to describe any outdoor prayer which links to the geographic location in which the prayer is prayed. Or as it is sometimes put, 'praying on-site with insight'. Three ways of prayer walking are:

- prayer-wandering. This is a personal time with God, chatting to him as we walk with him through his creation.

- prayer-watching. This is visiting an area specifically to ask God to reveal something to us as we watch and listen.

- prayer walking. This is structured prayer that 'covers' the ground, seeking to bring focused prayer into a particular area, often involving several people.

In the remainder of this chapter we explore each of these styles of prayer walking in more detail, providing an explanation and some practical pointers.

Prayer wandering

Jesus often withdrew to lonely places to pray (e.g. Lk. 5:16). We too can find that our prayer times take on a freshness as we withdraw to spend time walking with God in a particular place, away from the distractions of our everyday lives.

If we walk in a particularly beautiful place, when distractions come, our eye is caught by fresh new elements of God's creation and this can help bring the mind back to prayer. If we walk in a busy place, we can be struck by a particular need for prayer and again, our minds are drawn back into prayerfulness.

Wandering in prayer can provide the space and freedom to allow our minds to escape from the things that occupy them on a daily basis and focus them on God. Praying for a longer period of time can be much more difficult than praying for a shorter one. Consider a discussion with another person. In a short conversation, we tend to focus more on the subject at hand than on the person we are with. As we spend longer with them, we become more focused on their character and person than on the particular theme we are discussing, which may move from topic to topic.

We may well find that our mind strays from God and from our prayer. That's only to be expected! When we walk with another person, our minds will flit from time to time to other subjects, as our conversation meanders. We then need to refocus our thoughts on our conversation with our fellow walker. As we pray, our minds wander and we need to bring them back to God and refocus on our prayer.

Prayer wandering is primarily an individual spiritual discipline, which begs the question as to why it is included in a book of resources on developing the corporate prayer life of a church. Its inclusion is partly on the grounds of completing the resources on prayer walking, but also to encourage the development of individual spirituality that will help the development of corporate spirituality. It is likely that the majority of growth in prayer will take place in individuals' prayer lives and thus it is vital to nurture such growth for a church to grow in its corporate prayer life.

Prayer Wandering

Psalm 23 offers a number of useful pointers for prayer wandering. David wrote this psalm from his early experience wandering out in the pastures looking after his sheep.

The Lord is my Shepherd. Allow the Lord to shepherd you through your prayer wandering. Rather than setting the agenda and bringing to the Father the things on your mind, try to allow God to shepherd your thoughts and prayers.

He makes me lie down in green pastures. He leads me beside quiet waters. He restores my soul. Be willing to spend some time resting with God as you wander. Allow God to work renewal and restoration within you.

Even though I walk through the valley of the shadow of death, I will fear no evil. As you walk and wander, if it feels appropriate, allow God to make you aware of the fears and anxieties that trouble you and bring them before him. Sharing them with him allows him to work his healing and comfort: **your rod and your staff, they comfort me**.

You prepare a table before me in the presence of my enemies. You anoint my head with oil; my cup overflows. Amidst all our troubles the Father brings the goodness, blessing and protection that a Father desires for his children. If God leads you in this way, become aware of the way that God has blessed you.

Surely goodness and love will follow me all the days of my life. Become aware of the Spirit's presence with you, bringing God's goodness and love into your life. Appreciate this as you walk.

I will dwell in the house of the Lord for ever. What God promises is eternal. What this world offers is short term! As you wander, try to allow your heart and mind to move onto Kingdom thoughts. One day we will have no other thoughts than these! Wandering in a place of solitude can help remove the distractions of our day-to-day lives in order to help us to glimpse the eternal.

Prayer Watching

The prophet Habakkuk cries out to God about what he saw in the world around him. He sees violence, injustice and conflict. The wicked seem to be winning and the righteous are hemmed in. But in Chapter 1 verse 5, God answers with an amazing promise that he will act:

'Look at the nations and watch- and be utterly amazed. For I am going to do something in your days that you would not believe, even if you were told' (Hab. 1:5).

Prayer watching is a particular type of prayer walking. It is where we look at a particular place and see what God sees and identify where he is at work. Rather than praying fervently for a particular place, let your observation and listening drive your prayer. It is perfectly OK to spend time in silence, just waiting and watching. Don't feel the need to be 'praying' the whole time.

Prayer watching can be done on an occasional basis or it can be done regularly for a sector of your local community. It offers a fantastic training opportunity in seeing the world as the Father sees it. Sitting in the same place, for a number of weeks or at different times of day or night, can add many additional spiritual insights to those you picked up on the first visit.

There are three key points to remember when prayer watching:

i **Observe now, pray later!** Your primary task is to watch and listen, rather than to pray immediately for the situation you see. In this way, God can show you more that you can pray about at a later time.

ii **Take time to acclimatise yourself**. At first, it may feel rather strange and you may feel conspicuous! Rest assured, you will blend into the landscape. Even when you are used to this, it will take time to settle down into prayer watching.

iii **Record your observations**. You may find it helpful to have a notebook to jot down thoughts for later prayer. If you are to revisit a place on a regular basis, having notes from a previous occasion may be very helpful.

EIGHT PLACES TO PRAYER WATCH

1   **In a shopping centre**: sit in a café or on a bench and watch the world go by. Try to see people as God sees them – precious and loved by him. Listen to what he may be saying and pray for them as they pass.

2   **In a railway station**: again, find a bench or seat, where you can observe people coming and going. When a train comes in and people come past, pray for them, watching and listening.

3   **On a bridge over a motorway or busy road**: stand and watch the traffic go past. Look at the occupants of cars and lorries and see what you can discern about them. Look around at the world that they are passing quickly through. Listen and watch.

4   **In your office or place of work**: if you can find time to do this without being accused of slacking, then pause and observe. Try to see your workplace as God sees it and pray for your colleagues as the Lord directs your heart.

5   **From a high point**: find a hill or go to the top of a tower or car park and look around you. Zoom in on certain buildings and ask God to show you what is going on in that place. Let that then guide your prayer.

6   **On TV**: watch a news bulletin with a different mindset. Rather than seeking to find out the news, focus on the news as a prayer watching exercise. Rather than immediately offering prayers of intercession for the items on the news, try to see what God feels and thinks about the news item.

7   **In a traffic jam**: spend the time looking around you, seeing fellow travellers and reflect on how God sees them. It beats getting frustrated!

8   **From the kitchen or lounge window**: look at your usual view but in a new light. See your neighbourhood as God sees it and ask God to show you the needs of your area.

Prayer Walking

Prayer walking allows us to soak a particular part of our neighbourhood with prayer, focusing on a few streets at a particular point in time. This is different from prayer wandering, where we free ourselves from distractions to enable us to communicate with God more clearly. In prayer walking, we seek to bring before God the needs of a locality in intercession.

It is best done by one or more small teams, although it can also be done by individuals. Your prayer can cover a range of areas:

- Prayer for every person and household to come to faith. Pray specifically for those known by name to members of the group. Pray more generally for those none of you know.

- Prayer for the community and the values that they hold. Pray for the care and compassion that exists within the community, one member for another.

- Prayer for the witness of the church in that locality. Pray for how the church is perceived, for its work and its outreach. Bring before God Christians who are known to be living in the area.

- Prayer for other specific needs as you feel led. You may be prompted by seeing particular buildings or by observing people or things that happen around you.

Keep prayer walking low profile and natural – just a few friends walking together through a neighbourhood. As you walk, also be open to what God may prompt you with. Invite the Holy Spirit to reveal things to you as he guides your steps and your prayers. Try to pray with purpose, but with excitement and a sense of working in collaboration with God.

Sometimes, you may feel that prayer walking is hard work. Satan seeks to oppose those who will bring prayer into the streets. Don't be afraid of this – in God we have the victory. Remember, as Jehosophat did, the battle is not ours but the Lord's (2 Chr. 20:15). You may find it helpful to remember the armour that God provides – five defensive pieces, plus the word of God (Eph. 6:14-17).

TWELVE TIPS FOR GROUP PRAYER WALKING

1   **Get yourself right with God**. Joshua told God's people as they were about to cross into the promised land, 'Consecrate yourselves, for tomorrow the Lord will do amazing things among you' (Josh. 3:5).

2   **Research the area** – try to find out as much as you can about the area you will be prayer walking – how many church members it has, what kinds of activities go on in the area, etc.

3   **When you meet, start with prayer**.

4   **Walk in teams of two or three**, (possibly four, but that is the maximum).

5   As you walk and pray, **pray with your eyes open** so you can see what is happening around you.

6   **Use Scripture in prayer**. Hebrews 4:12: 'For the Word of God is living and active'.

7   Don't be afraid to watch and **be silent** for a time as you pray.

8   When you meet people, **smile and be open**. If you engage with people, be willing to admit what you are doing.

9.   **Keep your prayers simple** but focused and specific.

10   **Pray again as a team at the end of your walk**.

11   Spend at least **a moment or two reviewing** your prayer walk. What do you feel was most significant about it?

12   Keep a **prayer notebook** and make entries the same day as you do the prayer walk.

Prayer walking need not take long – between half an hour and an hour is plenty of time to walk around a small area. Done regularly, you can soon build up the area you cover.

CHAPTER TEN
Prayer Events

Whilst regular prayer groups are important, it is also appropriate to bring focused prayer onto particular situations at certain times. Holding a prayer event is one way of doing this. A prayer event is like a concert, meeting or conference – it is a gathering of people to achieve a certain aim. The event could be an outwardly visible one such as a prayer walk or an open-air prayer meeting or it could be a more discreet event in a central venue.

Constructed and presented in the right way, these events can draw people who might not otherwise come to a prayer meeting. However, to achieve this, the organisers will need to decide the answers to several questions:

- What is the purpose of the event?

- What is the broad structure and style of the event?

- How many people are likely to attend?

- What is the best venue for this? Is it a visible event or not?

- How can this be communicated so that it will attract people to come?

The event will need to be planned like any other event. Getting the organisation and logistics right are vital for the event so that the prayer flows smoothly. You may like to separate out the roles of event organiser and prayer leader to ensure that the logistics don't conflict with the preparation of the prayer time.

This kind of event can be a great way for churches to come together in a locality to pray and work together. However, this is likely to require a longer planning period.

HERE ARE SOME SUGGESTED PRAYER EVENTS

■ **Prayer breakfast**: a prayer breakfast is a popular way of getting people together to pray. Perhaps between 8am and 10am, this allows 45 minutes or so for people to talk and build relationships over breakfast before engaging in a time of worship (maybe 15-20 minutes) and then prayer. The thoughts in Chapter Eight may be helpful on planning the prayer time.

■ **Prayer walk**: people gather together in a central venue and engage in a time of worship before walking around the locality, praying as they go. Unless this is an act of witness (see below) and it is clear to people passing what you are doing, this is best done in smaller groups, of threes and fours.

■ **Prayer walk of witness**: unlike the previous event, where you pray as you walk, here it is best to pray at certain points along the route or at the start and end of the walk. During the walk itself it can be helpful to sing or have some other music. Good Friday can be a popular choice for such a walk, perhaps with a big cross at the head of the procession.

■ **Prayer concert**: a gathering in a central venue for worship and prayer. There will be a number (six or seven?) of interludes of Christian music, which those attending may join in or they can simply listen. In between these are prayer slots where people form into small groups, following a briefing from the front. These times of prayer should be kept to about ten minutes. Again, the material in Chapter Eight may be useful in preparing these briefings.

■ **Prayer pilgrimage**: travel or walk to certain places to pray, perhaps around the ancient bounds (or boundaries) of your parish or district. Alternatively, you could visit each school or church, pausing to pray at each one. A team from The Teal Trust who produced this booklet undertook a pilgrimage to pray at one church in each of the 42 English Dioceses of the Church of England in 24 hours. During a fantastic experience, we met with God around the clock in all sorts of different church settings.

CHAPTER ELEVEN
Prayer for leadership

Jesus said, 'I will show you what he is like who comes to me and hears my words and puts them into practice. He is like a man building a house, who dug down deep and laid the foundation on rock' (Lk. 6: 46,47).

Prayer was the foundation of Jesus' ministry. Before his ministry started he spent forty days in the desert preparing himself. Frequently he would withdraw to pray, to spend time with the Father.

Prayer is no less vital for God's church today. Our leaders not only need to spend time themselves in prayer, but also to receive prayer support from within the church. We know that we will need quality time in prayer to become tuned in to where God is moving, if we are seeking to be obedient to his call and direction. At the same time, Christian leaders are under greater and greater pressure as they minister to a society which itself is under pressure. Leaders need to be men and women of prayer, seeking the Lord in all aspects of their work. Yet they also need to be supported in prayer, by the church community and by those whom God may be calling to intercede for them and for their ministry.

As a first step, leaders need to acknowledge their need for prayer support, to ask the Lord to provide them with intercessors who can 'stand in the gap' on their behalf (see Ezek. 22:30) to present their needs and ministry before the Lord. There are several reasons why this may not be as easy as it sounds:

1 **Leaders may not realise how much they need prayer support**. Things may be going OK – but how much better could they be? There has never been as much pressure on our leaders as there is today. Many Christian leaders need greater prayer support than they are able to provide for themselves.

2 **Leaders don't ask for prayer support!** After all, there are far more urgent needs out there – people in need of healing, a world torn apart by violence, those who are bereaved, etc. Even if the need for greater intercessory support for leaders is recognised, humility can often be a barrier to the ministries and work of leaders being presented as a

need for prayer. Yet it is a very healthy and positive Christian practice for others to engage in intercession for leaders.

3 **Our use of prayer often tends towards situations where there is a problem or healing is required**. Receiving regular prayer support may make the leaders feel that their ministry is inadequate or gives undue focus to areas in which the leaders are not strong.

A recent study of Anglican parish clergy in the UK by Yvonne Warren (*The Cracked Pot*, Kevin Mayhew, 2002) shows only 10% of clergy interviewed were in the top two categories of emotional strength (strong and energised), yet 47% were in the bottom two categories (stressed and falling apart). An earlier study amongst US clergy found 70% do not have someone they consider a close friend, 70% say they have a lower self image than when they started the ministry and 80% believe that pastoral ministry has affected their families negatively.

Whether or not these numbers are accurate figures for ministry as a whole in the UK today, there is little doubt that building up a network of prayer can help prevent some of the stress and pressure today's church leaders are likely to face.

Asking for prayer support and building up effective relationships with intercessors is not easy. However, we can learn from Paul. Throughout the epistles, we understand that Paul knew his need for prayer support, for particular crisis situations and for his ongoing ministry. He asked for prayer from the churches in Ephesus (Eph. 6:19), Rome (Rom. 15:30), Corinth (2 Cor. 1:11), Thessalonica (1 Thes. 5:25), Philippi (Phil. 1:19) and Colossae (Col 4:3). Paul's request to the Philippians for prayer highlights the high importance he places on intercession in deliverance from his imprisonment. In his letter to Philemon he is so confident that the prayers for his release will be successful that he asks Philemon to prepare a room for him! His requests in Ephesians and Colossians are for prayer for his ministry of proclaiming the gospel.

TWO PRAYER SUPPORT CHECK-LISTS

First, three questions for leaders to review the prayer support they are receiving for their ministry:

1 Review the level of prayer support you think you are receiving in your ministry. There may be some base level of support from church members praying for their leaders occasionally. Other individuals may have a specific call to pray for you as an intercessor. This review may lead on to prayer, asking the Lord to lead you to potential intercessors.

2 How do you feel about people praying for you? Do they have enough information to pray appropriately? This is likely to mean different amounts of information for different people.

3 Write down your three greatest needs for prayer. Who could you ask to pray for these for you?

Next, three questions for the church council or wider church to engage in as part of a review of prayer for the church's leadership and its direction. This discussion may best be chaired by someone other than the leader.

1 Is the leadership prayed for as an integral part of the church's corporate prayer life? If so, do prayer groups have enough information on the needs of leaders?

2 Does the whole church congregation receive regular encouragement to pray for their leaders as part of their personal intercessions? Do they need reminding of this?

3 Does your leadership need greater personal prayer support? If so, are members of the church council or the wider church prepared to commit themselves to provide such prayer support and to pray for the Lord to provide others to pray? They need not know whom God has called but only that their prayers have been answered.

CHAPTER TWELVE
Final thoughts

Prayer can have the power of an ever-flowing river, cascading down over mighty waterfalls; or it can be a dried-up stream in a barren desert. Focusing on the prayer life of the church, providing encouragement and support will help keep the water flowing. In a nation where Christianity and churchgoing are in long-term decline, it seems natural that encouraging the prayer life of our churches should be a major priority. Yet observation of a good number of churches across the country suggests that corporate prayer may not have this priority.

If we believe that God has given Christians the gift of allowing us to present our needs to him, then surely prayer must be one of the most powerful ways of reversing the decline in churchgoing, bringing new people to faith and changing the priorities and values of our society.

This will not happen by accident! We will need to focus on building up prayer, teaching about its importance and encouraging people to pray in different contexts. Perhaps most of all we can encourage this by allowing people to discover that God is waiting to meet with them in a very real way, and not only to meet with them but to respond to the needs and concerns that are presented to him.

Throughout this short resource book, a number of thoughts and ideas on how to develop the prayer life of a local church have been presented. Not every idea will apply in each local situation, but hopefully you will have gained some thoughts and ideas that you wish to apply. It is our prayer that God would bless you as you seek to move ahead with implementing these.

We hope this short guide has provided a useful stimulus to help you review and nurture the prayer life of your church. If you have been challenged by it and need help following through, please write to us and we will try to help. We'd also love to hear from you if you have experiences of developing prayer within your church, or other ideas or tips, that you'd be willing for us to share on the Prayerguide website.

Please contact us at :

John Preston,
Director, the Teal Trust,
11 The Evergreens, Sheriffhales, Shifnal, Shropshire, TF11 8SB.
E: mail: info@teal.org.uk

About the Teal Trust:

The Teal Trust seeks to encourage leadership and prayer through paper based and Internet resources, providing Livewires kits for schools and resourcing leaders in developing countries with leadership books. One of the most easily accessible methods of accessing our resources is through the web, where many of our materials are available without charge.

Christian Leadership World: www.teal.org.uk

PrayerGuide: www.prayerguide.org.uk

Teams: www.teams.org.uk

The Livewires Project: www.thelivewireskit.org.uk